T0182418

What Do We Know About
the Yeti?

by Ben Hubbard

illustrated by Manuel Gutierrez

Penguin Workshop

For Malc, Tom, and Smit: FM—BH

For those of you who like to know about
all these mysterious creatures—MG

PENGUIN WORKSHOP
An imprint of Penguin Random House LLC, New York

First published in the United States of America by Penguin Workshop,
an imprint of Penguin Random House LLC, New York, 2024

Visit us online at penguinrandomhouse.com.

Library of Congress Cataloging-in-Publication Data is available.

Printed in the United States of America

ISBN 9780593752111 (paperback)   10 9 8 7 6 5 4 3 2 1 CJKW
ISBN 9780593752128 (library binding)   10 9 8 7 6 5 4 3 2 1 CJKW

Contents

What Do We Know About the Yeti?

At around 4 a.m. on September 22, 1921, explorers found mysterious footprints near the world's highest mountain. By the light of a bright moon, the tracks were large, and led up a snowy pass ahead. The team was high in the Himalayan mountains, close to 21,000 feet above sea level. Few animals were known to live at this altitude (height)—especially ones with such big feet! The climbers wondered if the tracks had been made by a gray wolf.

The explorers were part of a British expedition to find a way up Mount Everest. At 29,032 feet above sea level, Mount Everest has the highest peak on Earth. It is a dangerous place. The mountain is made up of dizzying slopes of rock and ice, where temperatures can drop to minus seventy-six degrees and winds gust at over

100 miles per hour. That's like the South Pole in winter. No one had yet found a way to the top of Everest. However, the mountaineers in 1921 believed they had discovered a new route. It was a snowy pass called Lhagba La that was located along the southern border of Tibet. This was a remote place that few people knew existed.

It made the discovery of the footprints even more curious. But the British team had no animal experts. They wondered what creature could exist in a place that was so cold and isolated.

Not everyone was puzzled by the footprints, however. Sherpas, expert climbers in Tibet and Nepal, were working as the expedition's guides and support team. They were skilled mountaineers who knew the area well. The team's Sherpas explained that the footprints belonged to a type of creature few had heard of outside the Himalayan mountain range. This creature lived in the mountains, walked on two legs like a human, and had long, matted hair.

When the team descended from the mountains, the Sherpas spoke to British journalist Henry Newman about the creature. Newman said that they called it Metoh-kangmi (say: MI-toe KANG-me), which means "humanlike bear of the snow." However, Newman decided to call it the "Abominable Snowman" (*abominable* means something unpleasant or horrifying). This was the moment that the legend of the Abominable Snowman was born. When British newspapers reported on the footprints, the story became highly exaggerated. One article in the *Times* of London had the headline "Tibetan Tales of Hairy Murderers."

But the climbing Sherpas had not described the creature as "abominable," or a "murderer." To them, it was simply a wild mountain creature that everyone in the Himalayas knew about. For people outside the region, what was now being

called the Abominable Snowman was a brand-new discovery, even though there was very little proof that it actually existed. The only evidence was the Sherpas' stories and some large footprints in the snow.

Was it real? Explorers would spend more than one hundred years trying to uncover the truth. Many have searched far and wide to find the mysterious creature we know today as the Yeti.

CHAPTER 1
The Local Yeti

After the 1921 newspaper reports, the Abominable Snowman developed a reputation as a savage, murderous monster with superhuman strength. It has held this reputation ever since. After all, it was right there in the name: "abominable," a word often used to mean brutal and beastly. But the people living in and near the Himalayas had a very different view. Their Yeti was certainly real, but not necessarily a violent people-killer.

The Himalayan mountains stretch for around 1,550 miles through Afghanistan, Pakistan, India, China, Bhutan, Nepal, Tibet, and Myanmar. Nepal and Tibet are the places most associated with the Yeti. The Himalayas contain ten of the world's fourteen highest mountains! At altitudes above 16,000 feet, the tops of the mountains are covered in snow and ice year-round.

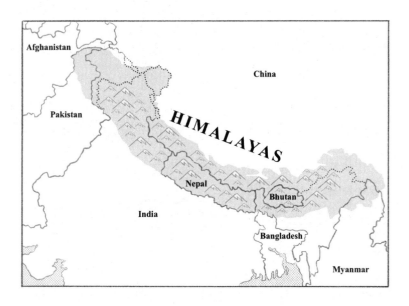

This freezing environment is difficult to survive. Only a few animals, such as snow leopards, brown bears, and yaks, can live at such heights.

Below the snow line (the altitude above which snow is on the ground for most, if not all, of the year), the Himalayan landscape changes. On the lower mountains and valley floors there are forests, shrublands, grasslands, and alpine meadows. The wildlife here includes monkeys, red pandas, goat antelopes, deer, bears, and even elephants in some parts of Nepal.

It is among Nepalese Sherpas that the word Yeh-teh (say: YEH-tay) first appeared. This is where the modern word "Yeti" comes from. *Yeh-teh* roughly means "cliff-dwelling bear," although there are two types of Yeh-teh. The first one is known as Dzu-teh (say: ZOO-tay), or "livestock bear." It walks on four legs, preys on goats, cattle, and yaks, and looks like a Himalayan brown bear.

Himalayan brown bear

The second type of Yeh-teh goes by the name Meh-teh (say: MEH-tay), or "human-bear." It is apelike in appearance and can be more than eight feet tall. It has long arms, a powerful chest, a conical head, and brown or reddish hair covering its body. It has a hairless face and flat nose, and can move on two or four legs.

However, it commonly walks like a human. Its feet have five toes, including one round big toe.

In some parts of Nepal, this Yeti is also called Nyalmo (say: NI-alm-o), Dremo (say: TAY-moo), and Chemo (say: KEM-o). In central Tibet it is sometimes called Migoi (say: ME-goy). In China the Yeti is known as the Yeren (say: YEAH-rin).

These are just a few of the names used for the upright-walking type of Yeti. Different Himalayan countries have their own names for it.

Statues of the Yeti in Shennongjia, China

People in the Himalayas believe the Yetis live in forests below the snow line. During the coldest months of winter, Yetis are thought to move to lower altitudes and close to human settlements.

They steal food from these settlements and also eat mosses, frogs, and mouse hares (also called pika). Yetis are rarely spotted and thought to be nocturnal (that is, they hunt at night and sleep during the day). Some Bhutanese people even believe that Yetis have the power to become invisible! A lack of sightings doesn't mean they can't be heard. People have said that they make a piercing whistling sound, similar to a high-pitched scream.

The Yak

The yak is a long-haired oxlike animal that lives on the high plains of Tibet. Related to the cow, the yak has a humped back, large horns, and a shaggy coat. Wild yaks are a black-brown color and can weigh up to 2,200 pounds.

Centuries ago, the wild yak was domesticated (tamed) by the Tibetans. The domesticated yak is smaller than its wild cousin, has a longer coat, and can be red, brown, black, and white. This yak is used for its meat and milk and also to carry heavy loads. Yak skin and hair are used to make rope, clothes, tents, and blankets. Some people believe yaks have sometimes been mistaken for Yetis.

Yetis can be seen in the artwork in Buddhist monasteries in Nepal and Tibet. Here, the Yeti is often depicted as a smiling, friendly creature. Some paintings show a "Yeti realm": a place between the worlds of humans and animals. Many Himalayan people believe the Yeti is both a real, physical animal and a spirit, similar to a ghost. There are Himalayan stories about Yetis that are hundreds of years old. These are recorded in monastery texts, which also describe the mythical origins of Tibet.

A thirteenth-century Tibetan Buddhist text called the Mani Kambum (say: MAN-ye bu-KA-bum) says that Tibet was once inhabited by creatures that were a mix between humans and monkeys. They had flat faces, were covered with hair, and walked on two feet. This story says that over time, these creatures evolved into the modern Tibetan people. But some stayed as wild, hairy people: the Yetis.

Buddhist Monasteries

Buddhism is a religion that follows the teaching of the Buddha, a holy man who lived in India sometime between the sixth and fifth centuries BCE. Buddha's teachings are called "dharma," and the most important are about wisdom, kindness, patience, and compassion. Buddhist monks usually wear long robes and have shaved heads. They typically live alone, or in monasteries, the buildings built to house their religious communities.

There are dozens of Buddhist monasteries in the Himalayan mountains. Each monastery is the home of monks, who spend their time praying, studying, and teaching Buddhism.

Stories from Tibetan folklore describe Yetis as being kind and gentle. These Yetis supposedly even cleaned the monasteries at night when the monks were asleep. In one famous story, a Tibetan mystic (someone who seeks a connection to a spiritual realm), called a Yogi, was wandering through the mountains. His leg began to hurt, and he soon found a hillside hut to stay in. On the other side of the hill,

the Yogi saw a large figure walking around. He went to investigate. In a crumbling shed, the Yogi found a Yeti lying on the floor. The Yeti had fangs, was covered with hair, and was running a fever. The Yogi then saw the Yeti had a swollen, infected foot. A sharp splinter was sticking out of it. Although he was afraid the Yeti would attack him, the Yogi removed the splinter and bandaged the wound.

A few days later, he saw the Yeti walk to the river to get water. At that moment the Yogi's leg was suddenly healed. As the Yogi walked toward a nearby monastery, the Yeti jumped down from a tree right in front of him. The Yeti carried a dead tiger on its back, which it gave to the Yogi as a present. It then ran away into the forest.

The Yogi arrived at the local monastery and donated the tiger hide (skin and fur) to the monks who were living there.

In another story, the Nepalese Lama (a high priest) Sangwa Dorje (say: SANG-wa DOR-gay) lived for many years in a cave meditating. A local Yeti cared for Sangwa Dorje by bringing him food, firewood, and water. When the Yeti died, Sangwa Dorje kept one of the Yeti's hands and its scalp (the top of the head, including the skin and hair). In 1667, Sangwa Dorje

Yeti hand

left his retreat and founded the Pangboche (say: PANG-bo-chay) Monastery. The Yeti hand and scalp were kept at the monastery as sacred objects. They were displayed during religious parades around the village. This practice continued until the hand was stolen from the monastery in the 1990s.

In these stories, the Yeti is a friend to humans. However, in other Himalayan folklore, Yetis are feared and avoided. Some Himalayan people believe that every mountain is a type of god, called a deity. If the mountain becomes angry with the people living there, it can punish them by sending out a Yeti, who is able to cause crops and livestock to die, or to capture and kill humans. People who believe in the mountain gods also believe that seeing a Yeti is a bad sign. Even photographing a Yeti could bring bad luck, or even death. These superstitions have made some Himalayan people cautious about the very idea of searching for a Yeti. Why look for trouble?

In European and North American cultures, however, finding and photographing a Yeti was seen as an exciting goal. After the 1921 reports, waves of expeditions began their treks up the Himalayas, hoping to find evidence of the truth.

CHAPTER 2
Sightings by Europeans

The 1921 sightings by the British climbing team were not the first time the Yeti had been reported to outsiders. In 1889, a British army doctor, Major Laurence Waddell, found some interesting footprints during a Himalayan expedition. Waddell thought they belonged to a creature mentioned by his Nepalese Sherpa guides. In a book about his experiences, he wrote:

"Some large footprints in the snow led across our track, and away up to the higher peaks. These were alleged to be the trail of the hairy wild men who

Major Laurence Waddell

are believed to live amongst the eternal snows, along with the mythical white lions, whose roar is reputed to be heard during storms."

At the time, Great Britain had great interest in exploring foreign territories. It wanted to claim additional lands and natural resources for the British Empire.

The goal was to colonize as many parts of the world as they could, which means to establish control over people and land for their own use. In some cases, it was also to conduct scientific research.

In 1859, British biologist Charles Darwin had published a famous book titled *On the Origin of Species*, which proposed a theory of how life evolved on Earth. It became accepted that humans evolved from primates, a group of mammals that includes apes and monkeys. But there were some scientists who thought that there must be a "missing link"—a creature that

Charles Darwin

had traits of both primates and humans—living in the wilderness. Perhaps it would look like a sort of ape, or wild man, covered in hair. Some thought it could be a Neanderthal, an ancient relative to humans. The description of the Abominable Snowman reported in 1921 seemed to ignite the hopes of these scientists. Interest in finding the creature increased greatly.

In 1925, Greek photographer N. A. Tombazi was exploring a glacier on the Himalayan border of Tibet and India for Great Britain's Royal Geographical Society. Tombazi was fitting a lens to his camera when he noticed the Sherpas on his team pointing to some bushes a few hundred feet below them. Here, Tombazi could clearly see a tall, dark figure standing in the snow. As he struggled to get his camera ready, the figure stepped behind the bushes and out of sight. Tombazi rushed to investigate and found footprints in the snow.

"They were similar in shape to those of a man, but only six to seven inches long and four inches wide at the broadest part of the foot. The marks of five distinct toes were perfectly clear," Tombazi later wrote.

Neanderthals

Neanderthals were close relatives to modern humans who lived between 430,000 and 40,000 years ago. They looked like people today, except shorter and stockier, with large noses and a prominent brow. Neanderthals hunted and gathered their food, and made simple tools from stone. It was once believed that Neanderthals were not very smart. However, recent discoveries show Neanderthals were reasonably clever. They created jewelry and had some language skills to communicate with one another. They were eventually replaced by *Homo sapiens*, early modern humans.

Although some people believe that Yetis could be Neanderthals who survived extinction and lived isolated in the Himalayas, there has been no evidence to support this theory.

Tombazi did not manage to photograph the creature, but his story fueled interest in the Yeti.

From the 1930s on, there were more footprint discoveries. In 1937, British mountaineer and botanist Frank Smythe found some human-looking footprints on a glacier in the central Himalayas. In that same year, British mountaineers H. W. Tilman and John Hunt also discovered footprints. It seemed that actually finding a Yeti might be likely. Then, in 1942, a stunning new sighting emerged.

Frank Smythe

Sławomir Rawicz (say: SLAV-o-mir RAR-veech) was a Polish World War II soldier who had been held in a prisoner of war camp in Siberia, in Russia. In late 1941, Rawicz and six others escaped and made a four-thousand-mile trek to freedom. This took them through the Gobi Desert in China and over the Himalayan mountain range. As they crossed from Tibet into India, the men saw two black specks against the snow. Thinking

Sławomir Rawicz

that these might be animals to hunt, the men moved toward them. When the men were about a hundred yards away, they sat down to observe the creatures. These were unlike anything the men had seen before. They walked on hind legs, were about eight feet tall, and were covered in reddish fur. The men observed them for nearly two hours, as the creatures didn't seem to mind them being there. Years later, Rawicz described the experience in his book, *The Long Walk*:

"Their faces I could not see in detail, but the heads were squarish and the ears must lie close to the skull because there was no projection from the silhouette against the snow. The shoulders sloped sharply down to a powerful chest. The arms were long and the wrists reached the level of the knees. . . . They were doing nothing but move around slowly together, occasionally stopping to look around them like people admiring the view."

By the 1950s, the rising number of Yeti sightings captivated people in Europe and beyond. But there was a second reason for interest in the Himalayas: conquering Mount Everest. Every country wanted to be first to reach the top of the world's highest mountain peak. Increasingly, these two points of interest seemed to overlap: As more climbers sought to find a way up Everest, more Yeti sightings were reported.

Mount Everest

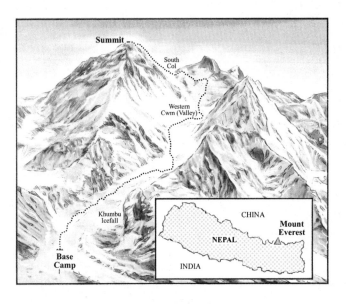

Standing in the Himalayas between Nepal and Tibet, Mount Everest is the highest mountain on Earth. Everest is 29,032 feet tall and covered with snow and ice. Near Everest's peak, the air is thin, the winds strong, and the temperature is constantly below freezing. This is known among climbers as the "death zone."

Conquering Everest became an obsession with mountaineers in the nineteenth century. Today there is a whole tourist industry dedicated to climbing the mountain. This has led to occasional human "traffic" jams on the mountainside, and to piles of garbage that climbers throw away on their way back down.

One famous example of the increased sightings occurred on Great Britain's 1951 Mount Everest Reconnaissance Expedition. Leading the expedition to find a route up Everest was English mountaineer Eric Shipton. He collected what would become the most famous proof of the Yeti. This was a photo of a Yeti footprint, taken next to a climber's pickax to show its size. The footprint was twelve inches long and showed four or maybe five toes, including one round big toe. It had clearly not been made by the boot of another climber! Shipton took the photo after following a line of footprints he found 19,000 feet up on the Menlung Glacier near Everest.

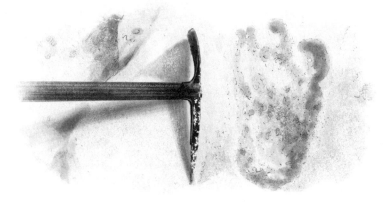

According to Shipton, the expedition's Sherpas told him the footprints belonged to a Yeti. They also said they had seen Yetis before, some as close as twenty-five yards away. These Yetis had conical heads, hairless faces, and were covered in reddish-brown hair. Shipton and the Sherpas followed the footprints for a mile, but had to stop because they were carrying heavy loads.

Eric Shipton's photo caused a great stir back in Britain. It was printed in the newspapers and examined by scientists. Some experts said the footprints proved the Yeti existed. Others were not so certain. After all, the footprints may have belonged to a different creature. Perhaps the snow had melted to make the footprints appear larger. Maybe someone had tampered with the footprints before taking the photo. Who could be sure?

In 1953, any news of the unidentified creature was overshadowed by a major event on Mount Everest. On May 29, New Zealand mountaineer Edmund Hillary and Nepalese Sherpa Tenzing Norgay became the first people to conquer Mount Everest. The news made headlines around the world. In the excitement, many people forgot all about the Yeti. However, both Tenzing and Hillary said they, too, had seen strange footprints during their Everest climb.

Edmund Hillary and Tenzing Norgay

Norgay and Hillary's report of footprints in the snow sparked the launch of the first full-scale search for the Yeti. Paid for by the *Daily Mail*, a British newspaper, the expedition was made up of a group of mountaineers, scientists, and journalists.

Edmund Percival Hillary (1919–2008)

Born in Auckland, New Zealand, Edmund Hillary might easily have become a beekeeper like his father rather than the world's most famous mountaineer. He discovered his love of mountain climbing when he was twenty and made a major climb up Mount Ollivier. He then served in the Royal New Zealand Air Force during World War II. He first traveled to the Himalayas in 1951, to join a mountaineering expedition in India.

In 1953, Hillary joined the expedition to conquer Everest. Near the top of the mountain, Hillary and Tenzing Norgay were chosen to make the final ascent—the climb to the summit. After scaling a forty-foot-high cliff face, the pair reached the top. They then planted the flags of the United Nations, Nepal, Great Britain, and India, and hugged, before beginning their long descent.

Edmund Hillary and Tenzing Norgay (shown
here) were the first to climb Mount Everest

This team would journey to the Himalayas to try to find a Yeti, capture it, and ship it back to London, England. This "Abominable Snowman Expedition" would last for fifteen weeks and employ 370 helpers to carry supplies, including a large cage. It would cost the equivalent of $1.2 million in today's money—a massive sum. In early 1954, the expedition set off for the Himalayas.

CHAPTER 3
Yeti Expeditions

The 1954 expedition sponsored by the *Daily Mail* began by visiting places where Yeti sightings had been reported. The Abominable Snowman Expedition quickly discovered new footprints in the Dudh Kosi Valley of Nepal. Team member Ralph Izzard even found one set of footprints that stretched out over eight miles! Izzard thought the nine-inch-long, five-inch-wide footprints belonged to two Yetis walking together. The footprints seemed to avoid human pathways and villages. However, Izzard later said it was possible different creatures

Ralph Izzard

made the footprints, which then melted in the snow. When this happens, snow collapses around an original footprint and makes it bigger. For this reason, some people believed that previously discovered "Yeti footprints" could actually have been made by wolves, yaks, or bears.

In addition to finding footprints, the Abominable Snowman Expedition collected samples to be tested back in British laboratories. These included hair specimens and animal droppings. But perhaps the most exciting Yeti sample was found in Nepal's Tengboche (say: TENG-bo-chay) and Pangboche monasteries.

Tengboche Monastery

Perched on a craggy hilltop at a height of 12,689 feet, the Tengboche Monastery has a view of Mount Everest. Inside the stone monastery, the expedition members found paintings of the Yeti. Some showed the Yeti called Meh-teh, which was covered in blue and green hair. Others showed the Yeti called Dzu-teh, which looked like a bear.

The expedition Sherpas explained that the Dzu-teh was simply the Himalayan brown bear, sometimes called the red bear. Expedition members therefore wondered if the Meh-teh

pictured was simply the Himalayan blue bear—
which is actually black, not blue—in color.

The real prize, however, was found at the
Pangboche Monastery, the resting place of the
supposed Yeti scalp donated by Sangwa Dorje
centuries earlier. The members of the Abominable
Snowman Expedition were astonished by the

scalp. It had a conical shape, was
covered in a thin layer of black
and red hair, and looked like
half of a large coconut shell.
Journalists on the expedition
quickly sent telegrams to
their editors with news. On
March 19, 1954, the *Daily*
Mail published a story saying the Yeti scalp had
been discovered. The facts, however, were slightly
more complicated.

Yeti scalp

For a start, the monastery would not let the
expedition remove their prized scalp for analysis.

But they would allow for a few of its hairs to be cut off. These were taken back to London and examined. Scientists found the scalp's hairs were not from a Yeti but probably from a type of goat. When the goat skin was fresh, it had probably been shaped into the form of a scalp before it dried. This "Yeti scalp" now looked convincing enough to make people believe it was real.

To get more information about the scalp, members of the expedition decided to send some of the hairs to the headquarters of the London police, called Scotland Yard. The men included a list of questions with the hairs, which they hoped the police would answer. But the police seemed uninterested. Their reply said simply: "Sorry, we don't know this man at all."

With this, the Abominable Snowman Expedition came to an end. It had failed to find a Yeti, or any real evidence that the creature existed. However, the expedition had succeeded in making the Yeti even *more* popular among people who were daring enough to try to find one. This led the Nepalese government to begin charging for Yeti-hunting permits. These cost close to $500 (in today's money) per Yeti. One hunter who purchased a Yeti-hunting permit was an American millionaire, Tom Slick.

Tom Slick

Slick was a Texas oilman (someone who owned and operated oil wells) who spent his vast wealth searching for mythical creatures, such as the Loch Ness Monster. He mounted an expedition to Nepal in 1958 to try to capture a Yeti. The expedition was made up of a hundred people and their hunting dogs. The team members carried guns with tranquilizer darts, ready to shoot and capture a Yeti.

Tom Slick's 1958 expedition to Nepal

Slick's expedition roamed around the Himalayan mountains for many months. They sent back regular reports to newspapers in the United States. On June 17, 1958, a *Washington Post* headline about them read "Snowman Reported Eating Himalayan Frogs." On April 30, a *Boston Globe* headline announced "Americans Find Cave of Abominable Snowman."

Neither of these headlines was true. In reality, Tom Slick was no closer to finding the Yeti than other expeditions had been. However, in July 1958, he believed he had finally found proof that the Yeti existed. He telegrammed the *Boston Globe* to report the news. On July 26, the newspaper ran the headline "Expedition a Success, Proves Yeti Exists."

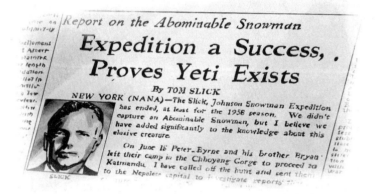

Report on the Abominable Snowman

Expedition a Success, Proves Yeti Exists

By TOM SLICK

NEW YORK (NANA)—The Slick, Johnson Snowman Expedition has ended, at least for the 1958 season. We didn't capture an Abominable Snowman, but I believe we have added significantly to the knowledge about this elusive creature.

On June 18 Peter Byrne and his brother Bryan left their camp in the Chhoyang Gorge to proceed to Katmandu. I have called off the hunt and sent them to the Nepalese capital to investigate reports

Slick had not found a whole Yeti, but instead part of one: a hand. This was the hand that Sangwa Dorje supposedly left at the Pangboche Monastery alongside a Yeti scalp. The hand, one of the monastery's precious artifacts, was mostly bone with some skin still attached. It looked humanlike. Slick was impressed with the hand, but wanted more than just to look at it. However, the monastery would not lend Slick the hand to take away, even for a large amount of money. So Slick decided to resort to trickery instead.

Peter Byrne

In 1959, a man named Peter Byrne returned to the monastery with a dried human hand given to him by Tom Slick. Byrne asked to see the Yeti hand in private and then removed one of its fingers. He substituted this with a finger from the human hand. He claimed he then gave the stolen finger to actor James Stewart and his wife, Gloria, who were in India at the time. The Stewarts agreed to smuggle the finger into England for analysis.

James Stewart and Gloria McLean

An analysis of the finger showed it was either human, or a very close relative. One possibility was that it belonged to a Neanderthal. There was no evidence that it belonged to a Yeti. Eventually, the finger went missing.

2 cm

Tom Slick died suddenly in 1962, but he had played a part in publishing and publicizing the Yeti story, especially in the United States.

The Yeti in Film

The Yeti first appeared on-screen in 1954, in

The Snow Creature. The movie features an apelike Yeti covered with white fur that hunters find living in a Himalayan cave. Next came *The Abominable Snowman of the Himalayas* in 1957. In this film, two Yetis covered in light fur and with humanlike faces are also discovered in a cave.

In 1964, an animated television Christmas special, *Rudolph the Red-Nosed Reindeer*, showed the Abominable Snowman as a giant apelike creature with white fur, named the Bumble. From then on, the Yeti was usually imagined as white or gray in the United States and Europe, rather than the reported red, brown, or black. In recent years, this white version of the Yeti starred in the animated movies *Smallfoot* (2018), *Abominable* (2019), and *Missing Link* (2019).

After conquering Everest, Edmund Hillary had maintained close links with the Sherpa people. Over the years, he would build schools and hospitals in Nepal. He was therefore a good candidate to lead a new Himalayan expedition. While the expedition was mainly to test humans' ability to adjust to high altitude, the group did some searching for information on the Yeti as well. Hillary investigated both the Pangboche scalp and hand (although he did not know at the time that one of the fingers had been substituted by Peter Byrne).

During Hillary's 1960 expedition, a new Yeti find presented itself. This was another supposed Yeti scalp, found in the Nepalese village of Khumjung (say: KUM-jong). Sherpas said the scalp was over 240 years old and was kept in the home of a local woman. Hillary asked if he could take the scalp for testing, but the woman said taking it away would bring bad luck. In the end, it was agreed to be sent to London by plane under the escort of the village headman, Khumjo Chumbi (say: KUM-jo CHUM-be).

Khumjo Chumbi said he had no doubt that the Yeti existed—he had heard one crying, and his children had even seen one up close.

The Khumjung scalp was analyzed in London, Chicago, and Paris, and found to belong to the Himalayan serow, a goatlike mammal.

Himalayan serow

Other skin and hair samples collected from Sherpas turned out to belong to brown bears. The expedition therefore concluded that the Yeti itself was most probably a bear. Hillary himself said he did not believe that the Yeti existed. And the scalp was returned to Khumjung.

Was Hillary right? No one had uncovered any evidence that the Yeti existed. But the people who lived in the Himalayas disagreed. For centuries they had believed in the Yeti and many had reported seeing them in the wild.

Whatever the truth, by the mid-twentieth century, the Yeti had found a place in the hearts of people around the world. Many believed in the existence of the Yeti. Some would even go to great lengths to prove that it was real. The search for the Yeti continued.

CHAPTER 4
The New Generation

The lack of evidence from the latest Edmund Hillary expedition did not discourage those who were still trying to find the Yeti. Instead, it created a new generation of explorers. Many had grown up reading about the footprint that Eric Shipton had photographed in 1951. Now, they, too, wanted to find proof that the Yeti existed.

One such expedition was mounted in 1972 by American zoologists Edward W. Cronin and Jeff McNeely. The men stumbled upon their first find while camping high in Nepal's Arun Valley, 12,000 feet above sea level. One morning, Cronin and Dr. Howard Emery awoke to see strange footprints between their tents, leading up into

the mountains above. The footprints were large and deep, and were clearly made by a two-legged animal.

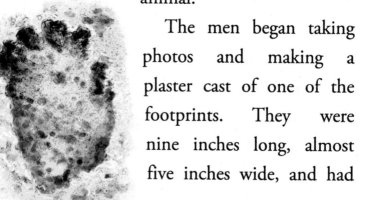

The men began taking photos and making a plaster cast of one of the footprints. They were nine inches long, almost five inches wide, and had one round big toe. Although a bit smaller, the footprints looked very similar to those found by Eric Shipton twenty-one years earlier. However, Cronin and Emery could find no other evidence of a Yeti, apart from the footprints. There were no droppings and no hair samples. The men stayed camped at the same place for a few days and explored the surrounding area. The Yeti, however, did not show itself.

Because the men were scientists, their discovery of footprints was taken seriously. Cronin's observations about the footprints also gained attention. He tried walking up the slope where the footprints were found, and discovered he quickly became tired in the deep snow. Before long he had to stop altogether. The Yeti must therefore have been extremely

strong to walk up the slope, and there was no sign that it stopped to rest. The depth of the footprints in the snow also suggested the Yeti was at least the weight of a grown man. Because the footprints were made at night, the Yeti was probably nocturnal. The Yeti was also clearly interested in the tents, as it had walked specifically over as if to see what they were.

Cronin thought this meant the Yeti may have been young, as older creatures would not have taken such a risk exploring an unknown camp. The tracks then led over the ridge and back down to the forests in the valley below, which was perhaps where the Yeti lived. However, Cronin found that the footprints matched no other animal living in that area. Perhaps, therefore, the visitor to their camp was one of a kind, Cronin concluded. What, then, could it have been?

Since the first reports of the Yeti emerged in 1921, many people outside of Nepal and Tibet believed it to be a type of giant ape. People living in the Himalayas seemed to agree with this description. American journalist Richard Critchfield spent time in the Himalayan mountains in the 1970s, around the same time as Edward Cronin. When asking Nepalese villagers to identify a Yeti, Critchfield found they were much quicker to point to pictures of a gorilla than a bear. He also learned that every one of them believed the Yeti existed.

Richard Critchfield

In the Nepalese village of Tashi Palkhiel (say: TASH-ee PALK-hi-el), Critchfield found eight men who claimed to have seen a Yeti while tending their yaks. One of the village elders described just such an encounter with a Yeti, which he called a Dremo. The elder said the Dremo charged at his yaks, grabbing one by the horns and breaking its neck. Other villagers said Dremos would eat a yak and then leave its skin on the rocks. This is how they knew one was hunting in the area. They also said that Dremos normally lived below the snow line, but sometimes moved above it in summer.

The villagers' descriptions of a gorilla-like animal fit with Edward Cronin's footprint observations. Cronin had wondered if the Yeti could be a type of giant ape. Scientists in London had also thought Shipton's footprints may have been those of an ape called *Gigantopithecus* (say: GIGANT-o-pith-e-kuss). *Gigantopithecus* was a giant ape that resembled King Kong.

Gigantopithecus

At nearly ten feet high, and weighing up to 1,100 pounds, *Gigantopithecus* was the largest known primate. It lived in the caves and forests of mountainous regions in China, Thailand, and India. In many ways, it fit with the legend of the Yeti. There was only one problem: *Gigantopithecus* became extinct around 11,700 years ago. Since then, no large ape has been known to have lived in the Himalayan region. However, this did not mean that one did not exist: just that one had not been found. The search for the Yeti continued.

In the mid-1980s, there seemed to be a breakthrough. A famous Italian mountaineer named Reinhold Messner became the first person to climb Mount Everest without using oxygen tanks. He had also conquered all the highest peaks of the Himalayas. During his climbs, Messner had always stated that he did not believe in the Yeti. But in 1986, he had an experience in Tibet that changed his mind.

Reinhold Messner

Messner was walking through a forest below the snow line when he saw a large figure before him. At first, he thought it was a yak. But then, without making a sound, it raced away from him, jumping over ditches and ducking under branches. The figure finally emerged in a clearing for a few seconds before disappearing again. After recovering from his shock, Messner crept forward. He soon discovered a footprint in the soil. It looked like a human foot, sunken deep into the soft ground. Messner took a photo and followed the trail of footprints further into the forest. Darkness fell. Then, Messner heard a terrifying whistling sound.

He saw the figure run behind a tree. It reappeared and stood looking at Messner in the moonlight. This is what he wrote happened next:

"Again, I heard the whistle, more of an angry hiss, and for a heartbeat I saw eyes and teeth.

The creature towered menacingly, its face a gray shadow, its body a black outline. Covered with hair, it stood upright on two short legs and had powerful arms that hung down almost to its knees. I guessed it to be over seven feet tall."

After gazing at Messner for a moment, the creature sped away through the trees. The encounter was quickly over. "No human would have been able to run like that in the middle of the night," Messner noted. He was in no doubt that the creature was a Yeti. And he became obsessed with finding another one.

For twelve years, Messner tried to prove the Yeti existed. He traveled through India, Tibet, Bhutan, and Nepal on his search. During this time, Messner visited monasteries and spoke to local people. He was told a Yeti hide was kept safe in the Gangtey (say: GANG-tay) Monastery in Bhutan.

Hanging from a wall in a dark monastery room, the hide seemed to be made from black hair and bones. As Messner took a photo, the flash from the camera revealed what he was really looking at. It looked like a monkey hide with several bones held in place by sticks. It had a mask in place of a face. To Messner, it was obvious the Yeti hide was a fake. But to the monks at the monastery it represented the idea of the Yeti as a spirit, rather than a physical animal.

Even though he completed many extensive searches, Messner did not see a Yeti again. But he learned a lot about the creature. This helped him come to a conclusion regarding the Yeti sightings. Messner decided the footprints found by explorers were actually made by the Himalayan brown bear.

Yeti National Parks

Both Bhutan and China have national parks dedicated to Yetis. In Bhutan, the Sakteng Wildlife Sanctuary greets visitors with the sign "Entering to Bigfoot (Megoe) Valley. Take only photographs. Leave only footprints." The name of Bigfoot on the sign is for tourists from the United States, where a Yeti-like creature called Bigfoot also inspires many passionate searches.

In China, the Shennongjia (say: SHAN-on-GEE-a) National Nature Reserve in Hubei Province is said to be the domain of the Yeren, the Chinese name for the Yeti. At the entrance to the reserve is a large statue of a Yeren and its young, indicating the boundary of Yeren country.

The Himalayan brown bear is a shy, nocturnal creature that often walks on its hind legs. It can weigh up to 880 pounds and reach over seven feet in height. The bear's coat ranges from sandy to reddish-brown in color. The bear also has large paws with five toes, just like many of the footprints found in the snow. For Reinhold Messner, the riddle of his Yeti sighting had been solved. However, this was only one person's opinion. Other Yeti hunters refused to give up their search for the mysterious creature they still hoped to find. And in another part of the world, brown bears walking upright were sometimes mistaken for the creature known as Bigfoot.

Bigfoot

Bigfoot—also sometimes called Sasquatch (say: SASS-kwatch)—is a large apelike creature that some people believe lives in the forests and mountainous regions of Western Canada and the US Pacific Northwest. The creature is described as between six and fifteen feet tall, covered in hair, and sometimes giving off a bad smell. Bigfoot sightings and footprints have been reported since the early nineteenth century.

Some Bigfoot enthusiasts and trackers believe it is a distant relative of the Himalayan Yeti. However, there is no proof Bigfoot exists. Today, it remains one of the world's most famous cryptids—creatures that are rumored to exist, although there is no evidence proving that they do. Other cryptids include the Loch Ness Monster, the Chupacabra, Mothman, and the Yeti.

The Loch Ness Monster

CHAPTER 5
Modern Theories

In the late twentieth and early twenty-first centuries, searching for the Yeti became easier than ever before. Less expensive flights and smaller video cameras meant that almost anybody wanting to find a Yeti could try their luck. Adventurers, amateur mountaineers, and television networks all mounted expeditions. New "Yeti footage" soon began appearing on US television shows such as *The Paranormal Borderline*. On one episode of the show, three experts reviewed footage called the "Snow Walker video." The video had supposedly been taken by a couple visiting the Himalayas in 1996. In the video, a hairy apelike creature is shown walking up a snow-covered hill. After watching the footage, the experts said they believed the creature was real. However, the show's producers later said the video was actually a hoax. The Fox network then showed the hoax video on a new show called *The World's Greatest Hoaxes: Secrets Finally Revealed.*

Image from the Snow Walker video

The Snow Walker video was not the only Yeti footage to emerge in the 1990s and 2000s. In 2007, a US television series called *Destination Truth* mounted an expedition to find the Yeti.

The crew filmed a line of thirteen-inch footprints found in the Himalayan snow. They also discovered some "Yeti hair," which was brought back to America for analysis. The hair, however, turned out to belong to the Himalayan serow. This was the same conclusion as with the scalp found by Edmund Hillary in 1960. It seemed most modern Yeti searches were coming to the same old conclusions.

In 2012, a British genetics professor named Bryan Sykes tried to solve the riddle once and for all. He asked for museums, scientists, and Yeti believers to send him samples they thought belonged to the Yeti. The DNA (the genetic material that makes up all animals) of the samples was tested against an animal database to see if they matched. The results were interesting. One hair sample from Bhutan was similar to another hair sample taken from the Indian region of Ladakh, in the western Himalayas.

Bryan Sykes

Sykes found that both samples matched the DNA of an ancient polar bear that lived in the Arctic around 40,000 years ago. Based on this evidence, Sykes thought it was possible that the Yeti was a mix between a polar bear and a brown bear. Over the centuries, the bear could have changed the way it looked and walked. However, more evidence was needed. "The next thing is to go there and find one," Sykes said.

Other genetic scientists disagreed with Sykes's findings and called for a new study. In 2017, the most in-depth study of Yeti samples to date was launched. It was led by Danish evolutionary scientist Charlotte Lindqvist, who analyzed nine "Yeti samples." These included

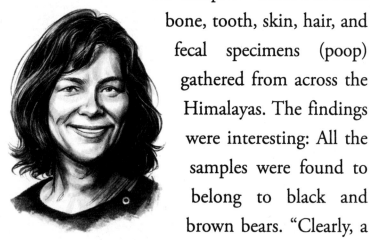

bone, tooth, skin, hair, and fecal specimens (poop) gathered from across the Himalayas. The findings were interesting: All the samples were found to belong to black and brown bears. "Clearly, a

Charlotte Lindqvist

big part of the Yeti legend has to do with bears," Lindqvist concluded.

However, there was a twist. The findings showed that the Tibetan brown bear is descended from the Eurasian brown bear. The bear probably migrated to the Himalayas thousands of years ago and developed in isolation up in the mountains. These bears would therefore have adapted over time to suit their new habitat. Perhaps this would explain the way the bears looked or moved—maybe in the manner of a Yeti?

Lindqvist's findings were disappointing for Yeti believers. Could the Yeti simply be a bear? One dedicated Yeti researcher thinks so. Daniel Taylor is an explorer who became fascinated with the Yeti after reading about Eric Shipton's footprint photograph. In the 1980s, Taylor traveled to the Himalayas to search for the Yeti, and then spent the next three decades trying to piece together the clues of its identity. He examined the historical evidence and explored the region. In 2016, Taylor published a book about his findings.

By examining the Shipton footprint alongside those of Himalayan bears, Taylor thought the large size of the footprint was caused by the bear stepping in one place with both of its paws.

This could have happened when the bear used its back paw to step into a footprint just made with its front paw. It would give the footprint its particular large shape. Taylor said the same thing probably happened with the Cronin footprints, except the snow was softer and the bear younger.

But what about the other Yeti descriptions, such as the terrifying whistling sound it makes? Taylor said this could be caused by the snow leopard, which makes a certain yowling sound.

Snow leopard

When this yowl bounces off the high Himalayan mountains, it could be mistaken for a whistling Yeti call.

In recent years, many explorers and scientists have come to agree with the bear theory. "Yeti samples" that include scalps, skin, and hair have been found to belong to other animals. Even Reinhold Messner, who wrote about coming face-to-face with a Yeti, later decided it was probably a bear.

And there have also been many hoaxes. An early hoax may have even been created by Eric Shipton himself. Edmund Hillary said Shipton could have made his famous Yeti footprint as a joke: "He [Shipton] was forever pulling practical jokes, fooling around in his quiet way. This footprint, see, he's gone round it with his knuckles, shaped the toe, pressed it in the middle. There's no animal that could walk with a foot like that! He made it up."

Others think that the Yeti was an ancient creature that has gone extinct—perhaps an ancestor to *Gigantopithecus*, or a relative of an ancient polar bear. Maybe it was somehow connected to the Neanderthals. Could it be possible that the people of the Himalayas saw such a creature hundreds of years ago and now it lives on as part of their myths and legends? After all, in the Himalayan region, the Yeti can be experienced as both a spirit and a real creature. But there is no definite physical proof that it exists. Yet.

The fictional large, dangerous apelike creature covered in white or gray hair that lived above the snow line is a version of the Yeti that we continue to see today. It is still often the image shown in movies, books, video games, cartoons, comic books, and other areas of popular culture. The idea of the white-haired, apelike Yeti seems to be here to stay.

This false idea of the Yeti has also created big business for certain Himalayan countries. In markets in Nepal, it is possible for visitors to buy fake Yeti fur and plaster casts of fake Yeti footprints. There are Yeti images that resemble the Abominable Snowman on clothes, toys, and many other goods for sale. In Nepal's capital, Kathmandu, tourists can stay at the Hotel Yak & Yeti and visit the Yeti Bar and Terrace at the Hotel Tibet. Yeti Airlines is the main domestic airline of Nepal.

Is there a real Yeti, somewhere still very high in the Himalayan mountain range, waiting to be discovered? Many believe so. Every year, people

flock to the region with the hope of seeing the elusive beast for themselves.

If you decide to travel to Nepal in search of the

Yeti, you'll have to follow three strict rules. First, you will have to pay the Nepalese government five thousand rupees (around thirty-eight dollars) for a Yeti permit. Once your permit has been granted, you'll be allowed to hunt the Yeti, and even capture it. But you must agree that you will not harm it. Finally, if you are lucky enough to find a Yeti, you must obey one last rule: You cannot talk to the press about it until you have permission from the Nepalese government to do so.

Good luck!

Timeline of the Yeti

1667 — Lama Sangwa Dorje donates a Yeti scalp and a hand to the Pangboche Monastery in Nepal

1889 — British army doctor Major Laurence Waddell discovers what he believes to be Yeti footprints in Nepal

1921 — British explorers find mysterious footprints in the Himalayas they say belong to an "Abominable Snowman"

1925 — N. A. Tombazi reports a Yeti sighting in Tibet

1942 — Polish soldier Sławomir Rawicz reports seeing two Yetis after escaping from prison in Siberia, Russia

1951 — British mountaineer Eric Shipton takes a famous photo of a Yeti footprint in the Himalayan Menlung Glacier

1958 — American millionaire Tom Slick undertakes a Yeti-hunting expedition in the Himalayas

1960 — New Zealand mountaineer Edmund Hillary leads a new expedition

1972 — American scientists Edward W. Cronin and Howard Emery report finding new footprints of the Yeti in Nepal

1986 — Italian mountaineer Reinhold Messner reports coming face-to-face with a Yeti

2017 — Scientists present an in-depth study of Yeti samples, such as hair, skin, and bone

Timeline of the World

1667 — The Russo-Polish War ends, with Poland giving up the eastern part of Ukraine to Russia

1889 — The Eiffel Tower opens in Paris, France—at 980 feet, it is the tallest structure in the world at the time

1921 — Adolf Hitler becomes the leader of the Nazi Party in Germany

1925 — The Tri-State Tornado, the deadliest in US history, tears through Missouri, Illinois, and Indiana, killing 695 people

1951 — Winston Churchill is reappointed prime minister of the United Kingdom at age seventy-six

1957 — The USSR launches Sputnik 1, the first artificial satellite, into space

1960 — Jacques Piccard and Don Walsh aboard the *Trieste* vessel descend into the Challenger Deep, the lowest point in the earth's oceans, to a depth of around 35,840 feet

1972 — The Watergate scandal erupts in Washington, DC, ending with the resignation of President Richard Nixon

1986 — The Soviet nuclear reactor in Chernobyl, Ukraine, explodes, causing a meltdown and the release of radioactive material across Europe

2023 — Five passengers aboard the *Titan* submersible (a type of submarine) are killed during a deep-sea dive to view the wreck of the *Titanic*

Bibliography

*Books for young readers

Coleman, Loren. ***Tom Slick and the Search for the Yeti***. London: Faber & Faber, 1989.

Coleman, Loren, and Jerome Clark. ***Cryptozoology A to Z***. New York: Simon & Schuster, 1999.

*Hergé. ***Tintin in Tibet***. American edition. New York: Little, Brown, 1975.

Hoyland, Graham. ***Yeti: An Abominable History***. Glasgow: William Collins, 2018.

Loxton, Daniel, and Donald R. Prothero. ***Abominable Science! Origins of the Yeti, Nessie, and Other Famous Cryptids***. New York: Columbia University Press, 2013.

Messner, Reinhold. *My Quest for the Yeti: Confronting the Himalayas' Deepest Mystery*. New York: St. Martin's Press, 2000.

Napier, John. *Bigfoot: The Yeti and Sasquatch in Myth and Reality*. London: Jonathan Cape, 1972.

Sykes, Bryan. *The Nature of the Beast: The First Scientific Evidence on the Survival of Apemen into Modern Times*. London: Hodder & Stoughton, 2015.

Taylor, Daniel C. *Yeti: The Ecology of a Mystery*. Oxford: Oxford University Press, 2017.